Watercolor

for the Artistically Undiscovered

by Thacher Hurd, John Cassidy

and _____

(Your name here)

Klutz Press Palo Alto, California

Write Us. Klutz Press is an independent
publisher located in Palo Alto, California and
staffed entirely by real human beings. We
would love to hear your comments regarding
this or any of our books.
Klutz Press, 2121 Staunton Court,
Palo Alto, CA 94306

Additional Paints and Paper.
See inside back cover.

Designed by MaryEllen Podgorski
Captions lettered by Colin Gooding
Production by Elizabeth Buchanan

Book is manufactured in Singapore.
Paints and brush in the United Kingdom.
Box in Taiwan.

Watercolors comply with ASTM D-4236

ISBN 1-878257-44-7

4 1 5 8 5 7

Table of Contents

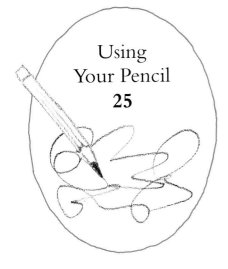

Introduction

Why You Can't Not Paint

Relax for a moment while we probe deeply into your mind and read your innermost thoughts. You're looking at this book and reading these words because, deep inside you, some little part of you would like to learn how to paint or draw. But, at the same time, you're confused, frustrated. Why? Because your artistic talent is in remission. It was last seen in a fingerpainted flower your mother stuck to the refrigerator. Since then, your genius has been in a deep sleep, perhaps even a coma, buried somewhere inside you. You haven't heard from it in years.

Allow us to make an obvious point.

Art is Personal Expression. You have YOUR talent. Nobody else has anything like it. They can't. It's biologically impossible. DaVinci splattered paint his way; you splatter paint your way. And looking at the *Mona Lisa* can provide you with many wonderful things, but it is no expression of yours.

In this book, the only mistake you can make is to criticize yourself, get in your own way—or to start straining and stop having fun. Your talent is for being you and for expressing all that wonderful you-ness; you're the world's absolute undisputed champion at it.

How to Use This Book

The book is divided into several categories. We cover the basics (Which end of the brush goes in the paint?) right here and in the first half of the book. The more technical points (light, shadow, perspective) are in the latter half. Although these technical points are the start of the process of learning how to work "representationally" (where you try to draw something *exactly* the way it looks), we don't talk about representational art in any particular depth because it's a subject well covered elsewhere, in more advanced books; and besides, we think it can be a little tight and limiting ("imitation world").

The Paints. As you may have noticed, a set of paints already comes with this book. These are opaque watercolors, made for us by Reeves, a division of the Winsor & Newton Company of England. They've been providing watercolors to the art supply trade for over a hundred and fifty years and they seem to have the technology down. We find their colors to be wonderfully satisfying and rich. We used them ourselves to do this book. If you're used to five-and-dime watercolors, we think you'll be very pleasantly surprised with Reeves paints. Incidentally, one of the colors you'll use the most frequently isn't in the palette. That would be white, the color of the unpainted paper. Use it often, and do so by deliberately leaving other colors off.

Watercolor paints in general are capable of leaving stains on clothing, although they will typically wash out. Use care and wear a smock, or clothing that could stand a little decoration. The paints are non-toxic, but even so, don't eat them.

Assuming you don't get into 6-foot wall murals, this set of paints should last for hundreds of paintings. Replacement palettes are available in art supply stores as well as our mail order catalogue (see last page).

The Brush. Brushes range in size from very tiny (number 000) to very large. As a compromise, we've included a middle-sized brush, number 5, with this set of paints. If you want to get an additional brush, we'd recommend a slightly larger brush. Never get really cheap brushes. They are horrible.

You'll also need an ordinary number 2 pencil for sketching when an outline is the first thing needed for a painting.

The Watercolor Paper. Since this is a working book, most of it is printed on watercolor paper (the rough, nonglossy pages). Watercolor paper is a special kind of paper that can take all the soaking it

gets. When you've filled up all the watercolor pages in this book, you're going to need a resupply of it. Ordinary paper won't do the job. You can find student-grade watercolor paper at large drugstores, discount places, office supply houses, and, of course, art supply shops. (Don't buy the most expensive kind; it's not worth it.) In addition, we carry watercolor paper in our mail order catalogue (see last page).

Why We Like Working Small

The paper in this book is nine inches square, but you'll have better luck if you don't try to fill single sheets with single, big paintings. Here in this book we recommend you work fairly small, or, at best, medium. An average page might end up with eight or nine "spot" paintings.

We have two reasons for this. Well, three, actually. One, your number 5 brush is the right size for working at this scale. Two, small paintings will get you more experience (per page). And three (the most important), quick, spontaneous strokes just happen more naturally at smaller scale. Big paintings take bigger brushes and (usually) more planning. Right now, at least, we don't want you to plan. We want you to paint.

Really Basic Watercolor Technique

Get a quart jar of clean water for washing your brush between colors. Then put a couple of paper towels beside the book, for blotting your brush.

Put the brush in your hand. Stick it in the water, then smush it around in one of the colors. Now, take a deep breath and plop it down on the watercolor page that faces this one. You're an artist.

Learning the brush. Take your brush for a test drive. Draw a long line and get a feel for how long a brushful of paint lasts. Then pick up the brush and wash it in the clean water. If you forget this and put it back into another color, making a mess, just clean off the top layer of the messed-up color with a bit of paper towel.

Get another color and draw some more lines. Learn what happens when you use a lot of water, and learn what happens when you use a little. Draw thin lines and thick. Draw wiggles and blobs. Learn how much pressure you need to get what size splat. When you're done filling the following three pages with splats, lines, wiggles, and smushes, and while you're letting them dry, take a second look. You are about to discover something wonderful.

All these line widths can be done with your number 5 brush. Just vary the pressure.

Push down hard on your brush. Let dry. Add claws.

A splat - line - splat - line - splat.
Push down hard, lift and repeat.

A twirl.
Push the brush
down to its heel
and spin.

ATTENTION: This is a learn-your-brush page.
Play and learn. Don't try to copy exactly.
You'll do better on your own.

Another Brush Play Page

Fill it with a dozen or so single
color loops, smushes, splats, etc.
Don't think. Just paint.

You'll learn how nice a quick,
spontaneous gesture can look.

Empty-headed loop and smush characters.
I didn't discover them until they were done.

More No-Thinking Brush Play

Try using more colors. Rinse your brush between color changes.

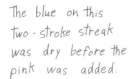

The blue on this
two-stroke streak
was dry before the
pink was added.

Quick, no-thinking strokes = clear colors.
Too careful, slow strokes = muddy colors.

11

One Last Page of Wiggles, Splats and Smushes

Do lots of them. Crowd the page. Don't try to create critters until you've read the facing page.

Like my 'do?

The Miracle of Discovered Art

Take a break from painting for a second and look carefully at your artwork. See if there isn't a WiggleCritter in one of your wiggles. Maybe all you need to do is push it in the direction it's already headed. So add legs, or eyes, or a moustache, or whatever.

Then look at some of your other lines, blobs, and splats. Maybe you see a flower. So add a stem. Maybe you see a cloud of steam. So add a cup. Maybe you see some footprints. So add the claws. The surprise and spirit that these happy (half-) accidents contain is one that very few pieces of calculated art will ever be able to match.

A warning, though: Don't strain this process. Some smudges are obviously leaning in some direction and should be pushed along. But a lot of them are perfectly happy as smudges and should be left alone in their smudgeness. This actually brings up one of our pet peeves and we will state it here and probably many times hereafter.

Thacher Hurd's Ironclad Rule of Spirited Watercolors

Watercolor is fragile. It will very quickly turn to muddy mush with a lot of revision, overworking, and massaging. The rule is this: **You're better than you think you are.** Your instincts and your thoughtless first strokes are spontaneous and spirited. Trust them. If you go back over your art too much, you'll pick it to death. Know when you've got a good thing and know when to leave it alone.

13

"Erasing" doesn't work so well.

before   after

What If I Make a Mistake?

You can't.

No, let us take that back. You *can* make a mistake. If you get critical of yourself and decide that something you've done is a mistake—*that's* a mistake. It *is* possible (kind of) to erase watercolors with a clean, wet brush or damp paper towel, but you'll never be able to get back to entirely white paper and besides, in order to erase, you've got to make a mistake. And that's impossible (see above).

Cut something out.

Splatter and Cut Page

Splatter this right page by snapping your brush, or pool up a little wet patch of color and chase it around by blowing through a straw. Use a lot of white and DON'T OVERWORK YOUR ART! When you're finished with both sides, get out a pair of scissors and cut this entire page up into smallish shapes (fish? flower? frying pan?). Learn how sizing and shaping with scissors can completely transform your work. Paste the shapes down on page 17 and then add a little line work around them, if needed, to complete the picture.

Like a lightning bolt...

Put down newspapers first!

Your Splatter Page

Do splatters on this page and its backside. Then get out your scissors and cut shapes—choosing between sides to find your favorite splatters.

Splatter Page

Another page destined for the scissors.

A smush wiped
with a paper towel

Technicolor
Meteor Shower

A splatter wiped
with a paper towel

Your Paste-Up Page

Paste down your cut-up pieces on this page.
If needed (and *only* if needed) add any
finishing touches with your brush.

A bowl of Italian splatter

Zoom-i-gator

A Stencil and Splatter Page

Using a big piece of scratch paper, cut out a few shapes (question mark, shoe, arrow, circle, starburst, etc.). Then firmly tape the stencil down on this page and splatter all over it. When the paint is dry, remove the stencil.

Cut a postage stamp stencil out of scrap. Tape it down and splatter away. Remove stencil when dry.

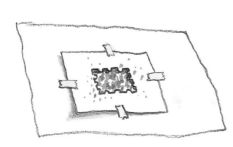

Your Color Experiment Page

Before you start in on this page, read the facing one.

This is no page to be timid. Put down a quick smush of color. Rinse your brush, and put down another color smush right by the first one, touching it. Watch how the colors marry. Fill this page completely with lots of little smushes.

Also, try this. Start with a patch of clear water, then dab a color into it. Rinse your brush, and dab another color into the water patch.

pink + black = purple

green + black = dark green

Rainbow:
Red, pink, blue, green, yellow.
One color at a time.
Do it quickly, so colors won't dry,
and they will mix together.

20

My Color Mix Pages

3 colors

Putting colors together is watercolor cookery, a matter of personal flair and taste. The few examples of color mixes shown here are just that—a few examples. The other 11,438,204 possible combinations of your six colors are not shown. They have been left for you to discover.

Wet Mixing. When you mix colors wet, they run together ("marry"). This is a wonderful technique and a wonderful time to remember the rule against overworking. Play with wet mixes to get a feel for them. Use your paper towel as a blotter when you want to dry your brush, or remove some color from it. If your paper warps because it has so much water on it, that's fine. That's what's supposed to happen.

Dry Mixing. If you don't want your colors to marry wetly, let the first color dry before you add another color to it (or even touch it). This takes a moment or two of patience, so you might try working on two pieces of art at the same time. One can be drying while you work on the second.

Wet on wet, dabbing pink on with point of brush

Wet on wet

Wet blue on dry pink

Colors and Color Combinations

See how black livens up your colors.

Do colors seem to jump out at you? Do some colors come forward and some recede?

Color Combining

Each of the boxes on the facing page gets two colors. Let each color dry before working next to it. At the end, look back over them all and decide for yourself how each color combination gets along. Note, at the same time, an important fact: Colors change depending on their neighbors. The very same blue (for example) can look darker, duller, brighter, redder, or whatever—depending on the color it's put beside.

Hot + Cold colors. Look at the four colors here and decide for yourself which you think are hot and which are cold.

Color Combination Boxes

 Instructions

Does the same green dot look different with different backgrounds?

Alternate two colors.

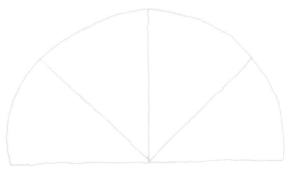

Do it again.   ...again.   23

Shapes (or, Trying to Stay Inside the Lines)

On this page, mix colors wet, dry, or in-between—your choice. Work quickly, freely, lightly.

Color TV test pattern

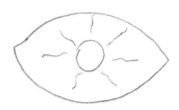

bloodshot eyeball

Tie-dyed T-shirt

ugly tie contest winner

Can't think of something to draw? Trace your own hand and color it in.

Playing with Your Pencil

Pencil work is often (but far from always) the first step in painting a watercolor. On this page and the next, outline shapes or objects first in pencil, then color them in. Use a light line and work sketchily. Wash some light color over the drawing.

The mummy walks!

Suggested subject matter: valentine heart, top hat, tire swing, wheelbarrow, lightning bolt, sailboat, →

More Pencil Play

Start with a pencil sketch, then go back
over it with light color.

Watercolor over pencil drawing.
I used the pencil almost
on its side, like this:

You get a wider line,
like this:

...butterfly, moon and stars, tropical fish, tree, quilt, fried egg, ghost, skateboard, billboard...

99 mph banana

Recess Time

This is a page to take everything you've learned and mix it all up in a big hodge-podge. Fill the page with a dozen or so spot pieces. Smear one with a paper towel, splatter another, frame some color with black for drama, put your thumb in the paint and leave your thumbprint. Use your pencil to outline a church window. Then fill it in. As always, work quickly, freely, happily. Your work will show it.

Thumbprint guy

Practice-Your-Wash Page

This is your practice page. Put your pencil away and read the facing page first.

Blue sky: A heavy blue line on top. Rinse brush. With clear water, wash blue down to cover whole box.

Blue sky alternative: A heavy clear water streak on top. Add blue. Wash downward.

Wet the whole box first with clear water. Then a heavy blue line on top. Touch with a pink line. Last, a yellow line. Work quickly.

Blue/pink sky: A heavy blue line on top. Next, a heavy pink line. One stroke each. Wash pink down.

Two colors (your choice).

Three colors (your choice).

Washes

Washes are at the heart of watercolor art. They are delicate, spirited and a bit unpredictable. Exactly like watercolor in general. As you'll soon discover, you can guide washes generally, but you cannot steer them precisely. That's what makes them so wonderful. *Caution:* Be quick and delicate. A single stroke of color is often all you need. Washes will die with overwork.

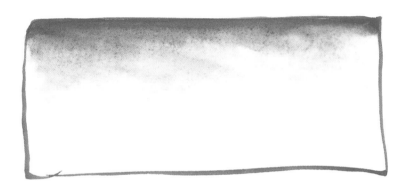

Blue sky. Here I laid a strong, thick line of blue across the top of the box. Then I cleaned the brush, blotted it, wetted it again and used it to "wash" the blue down to fill the box.

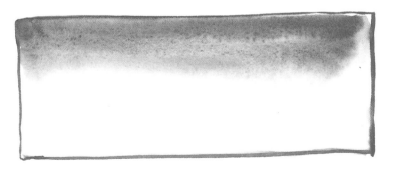

Another way to do blue sky: with a clean, very wet brush, I covered the whole box with water, really soaking it. Then a stroke of blue at the top and let it work its way down. The paint spreads by itself if the paper is wet enough.

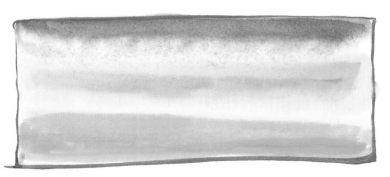

Adding a third color is mostly an exercise in restraint. I started with a blue streak, washed it down with a clear wet brush, then did the same with pink, and finally green. One or two strokes per color was all it took. Too much work and the colors will get muddy.

Soggy rainbow. Paper was wetted first with clear water. Then a quick stroke of green, then pink, then blue. Red at top was last.

I think I let the paint dry between colors here. In general, I start with the lighter colors (like yellow), but here I think the light purple went down first. So much for my rules.

Skies are darker at the top.

Multicolor washes went down first, black next, and stars last of all.

Wash Play

Fill boxes with one, two,
or three color washes.
For a rough idea, see
facing page.

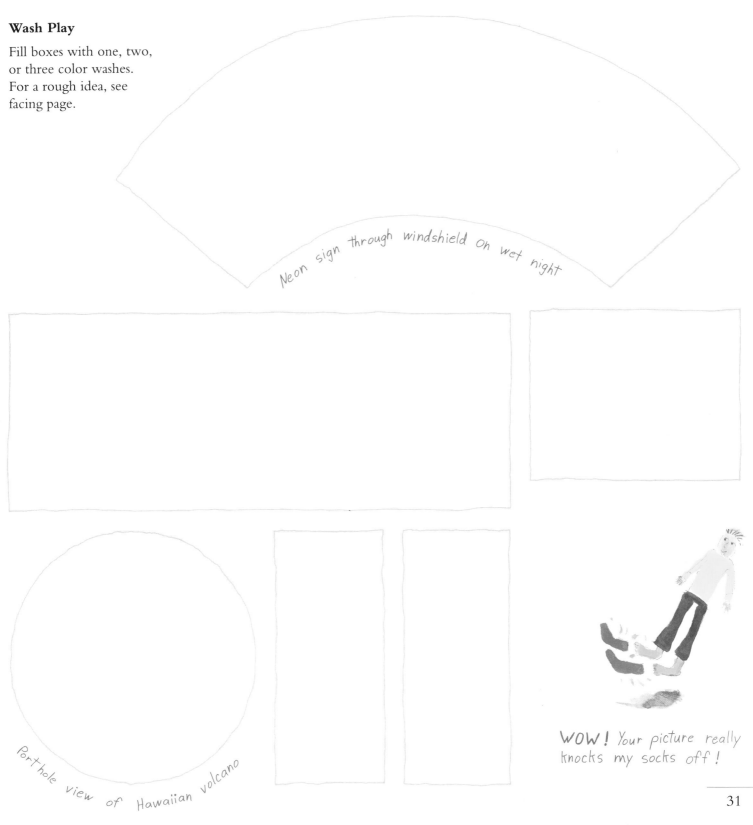

Neon sign through windshield on wet night

Porthole view of Hawaiian volcano

WOW! Your picture really
knocks my socks off!

More Wash Play

With your pencil, fill this page with shapes: boxes, circles, blobs, or whatever. Fill your shapes with quickly done washes using one, two or three colors. Don't try to plan them in advance. As you've probably discovered, washes aren't like that.

Suggested titles: Forest fire at night from distance, Single red cardinal in flock of blackbirds, Venus sunset, Bowl of fruit through aquarium, Lightning strike in storm, Stack of Christmas boxes,...

Wash and Crayon Play

Crayons are waxy, and will try to resist mixing with watercolors. On this page, you're going to use this un-mixability in an interesting way. The technique is simple: Do a crayon drawing and then *quickly* paint a wash right over it. Too much paint will overwhelm the crayon. Be quick and cautious. Additional watercolors can be added (use restraint!) either wet or dry.

Gator and bunny were only outlined in crayon. Everything else was watercolor and applied immediately after the crayon.

The comet was done first in crayon— yellow, pink and red. The black and blue watercolor were added last.

33

Landscapes

Watercolors have a texture and softness that lend themselves extremely well to landscapes. In fact, it's such a good fit between medium and subject matter that some watercolorists do nothing *but* landscapes.

More Landscapes

This time, draw your own framing shapes.

Evening in Kansas

Cloudburst

Suggested Titles: Foggy Low Buildings, Hills and Low Clouds, Crazy Daybreak, Stormy Seas, Prairie Fire, Buffalo Herd, Tornado in Nebraska, Lone Boat in Big Ocean, Fireworks at Sea, Distant Rainbow, Snow-Covered Peaks, Moonscape, North Dakota Ski Slope, ... →

Even *More* Landscapes

...Streaky Sunset, Rolling Wildflowers Purple Skies of Fantasy, People-Covered Beach Seen by a Swimmer...

Black and White Oddscapes

This is a page designed to take advantage of the power of black and white, and at the same time to show you how the shape of your watercolor affects it.

With your pencil, draw five or six shapes. (Suggestions? A low wide box, a tall skinny box, a keyhole, a circle, a half moon, a teardrop, an oval...)

Now, using only the black in your palette and the white of the page, fill the shapes with patterns.

Frumious Bandersnatch

a Frog Prince (before)

Popsicle Bird

Monday morning

Technicolor Beasties

Keep your beasties fairly small and use everything you've learned so far about shapes, washes, dry mixing, wet mixing, the Ironclad Rule and the value of thoughtless first strokes. These little beasties should be half-discovered, half-created. Do at least one of them while you're on the phone. If you work at a smallish scale, a page like this can end up looking like a mini-zoo from the Lost Continent.

Sclerotic Pouncemaster

Dancing Dewbabies

Nightmare O'Mine

a Knock-Kneed Flutterby

a Couple of Parameciums from Paraguay

Uranian Housepet

a Crayola Reptile

Still more beasties! Do *lots* of them!

the Dreaded Bet Nwar

the Munchkin Mistake

a Cubist Alligator

WOOF!*

*GREAT PICTURE!

a Cabbage Patch Gila Monster   Parrots on Parade   Black Panther at Night

Alphanumeric Art

Letters and numbers are the most common printed shapes of all, but within their common shapes lies a world of possibility. Your job here is to design your own alphabet and number set. Work mid-scale so you can get three or four versions on this two-page spread. Letter to letter, you should change the spirit from flashy to fancy to fussy to feeble to freaky to frowning to fishy to frenzied to flat to ...

N P O Q R V V W Z

8 9 10

Recess Time Again

Why not write five or six opening sentences to the Great American Novel ("It was a dark and stormy night...") and illustrate them all?

Through the brief opening in the clouds, Commander Jackson clearly saw the alien spacecraft, glowing pink and yellow.

Suggestions?

★ Call me Fish Mail. Everybody does. Maybe it's my gills.

★ Life isn't easy when you're a hammerhead shark who doesn't like seafood.

★ The sun rose bleakly over the Martian hills. Captain Xfftgr wrinkled his twelve brows and coughed weakly as he looked over his territory.

Light and Shadow

Put this book near a lamp or window.
Point your finger out and stick it
straight down onto this dot: ●

Now look at the shadow (or shadows) your
finger throws onto the page. Look particularly
at the edge of the shadow, where it fades into
nothing. Then find the darkest part of the shadow.
See how the shape of the shadow relates (or doesn't
relate) to the shape of your finger.

Then, look at your finger in a way you've probably never done
before. Look at it as a simple object blocking light rays. Where the
rays hit it directly, it'll be bright. Where they hit it indirectly, it'll be
shadowed. Note where the brights are the brightest, and where the
shadows are darkest.

This pattern of bright and dark is on everything you see, despite
the fact that you probably never pay it any attention except in
extreme cases where the light is strong and from a single direction
(like when you put a flashlight under your chin on Halloween
night). Light is what gives objects their shape.

Apple in a
dark room.

Apple in a room
with light.

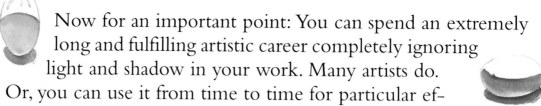

Now for an important point: You can spend an extremely long and fulfilling artistic career completely ignoring light and shadow in your work. Many artists do. Or, you can use it from time to time for particular effects. It can add a specific emotion to a piece, or it can add dimension and reality to it, if that's what the piece needs. It's a tool. Use it or not, depending on your taste and your goals.

You've seen shadows and light patterns so often in your life that you're not seeing them at all anymore. If you want to use light play in your work, you're going to have to re-open your eyes. So Step One is to look around you and examine everything for the pattern of light and dark. Ask yourself where the light is brightest, and the shadows darkest. Look particularly at the boundaries between light and shadow. This "turning edge" is where the shadows tend to be darkest.

Then, pick up your brush and begin playing with the exercises described on pages 45 to 48 to see if light play and shadow interest you, and if they do, incorporate them elsewhere into your work when you think it's appropriate.

light → →

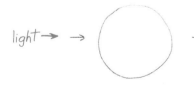

① Draw a circle.

② Squiggle at turning edge. A dark turning edge helps to give the illusion of solidity.

③ Soften squiggle.

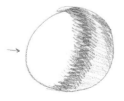

④ Darken shadow side.

⑤ Soften pencil lines lightly, and add shadow on the ground. Remember shadow is on opposite side from where light is coming from.

A Light and Shadow Coloring Page

Fill in these shapes, but imagine they are being lit by a single light bulb from the direction of the arrow. As always, work quickly. Too much planning and, worst of all, revision, can get you into muddy trouble.

→ = where light is coming from

Onward with Light and Shadow

Get out your pencil, draw your own shapes on this page and "illuminate" them from a single direction. As a help, set something in front of you (a book?) and turn a single lamp on it. Study the bright/dark pattern on it. Sketch it in pencil, then fill in with color. Sensitize your eyes to light and shadow!

Suggested objects? Bowling pin, pumpkin, cactus, rocket, boom box, bucket, tire, teakettle...

 light ⟶  ⟶

Bowls and cups are tricky. Set one up in front of you and study it.

Light and Shadow Extremes

By intensifying the light, you simultaneously deepen the shadows. Try some more shapes and simple objects on this page, but put them in a *bright* spotlight. Suggestions? Boot, box, balloon, bread, basket, bottle, boat... Change the direction of the light source.

Notice I erased the front edge of these shapes, but the eye doesn't mind.

Standing in a Pool of Light

You can "ground" an object, or give it some extra solidity, by smushing a little pool of shadow at its feet. Note that shadow has a *very* soft edge. If you harden the edge of a shadow, it looks more like ink than shadow. Keep it loose and smushy.

When the sun sinks low, the shadows are long, pardner.

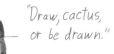

"Draw, cactus, or be drawn."

When the flashlight is high, the shadows are short.

Anatomy

As any art student can tell you, it's terribly important to learn proper anatomy. You need to learn where the nose is, what big teeth a wolf has, how skinny the legs on a bird are... things like that. With the importance of that in mind, here is your page for practicing body parts.

How the pros solve special problems:

Have a hard time
drawing eyes?

Can't draw hands?

Heads?

Like light and shadow, perspective is another tool to put into your skills kit. You can pull it out often, sometimes, or never. It all depends on your taste and goals. Rest assured that whichever you do, there are many artists who do the same.

Painters first began using perspective illusion about 500 years ago in an effort to imitate the appearance of the real world. The problem they were dealing with was this: Appearance-wise, the real world is a weird place, as you may have noticed. For example: You look down at the end of the block and see a human, moving its legs and slowly enlarging. Is this strange? It ought to be, but your brain takes it right in stride. Someone is walking toward you.

The Black Hole (Vanishing Point). Imagine that everything in your picture is being sucked into a tiny black hole at the center of your picture.

To mimic this strange phenomenon on a flat piece of paper, artists have developed a number of tricks, but the most fundamental one is this: To make something appear distant, make it smaller. Carry this rule to its logical conclusion and you'll see that very distant things are so tiny they vanish completely, just as they do in the real world. That vanishing act is translated onto the page in something called the vanishing point, which is a point you can actually put on the paper.

How to draw a highway to nowhere

Vanishing point

Start like this...

... and fill it in.

Let's take something ordinary like a can of soup.

Lay it down like this, and the bottom looks farther away than the top. Why? Because it is drawn smaller.

If you were to stick another can onto the bottom of this one, and then another to the bottom of *that* one, and so forth and so on for a million cans, you would draw them smaller and smaller until they finally disappeared into the distance—into the vanishing point.

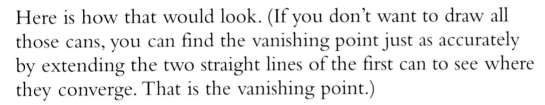

I million cans

Here is how that would look. (If you don't want to draw all those cans, you can find the vanishing point just as accurately by extending the two straight lines of the first can to see where they converge. That is the vanishing point.)

Here is the same "Where is the vanishing point?" exercise done with a simple house. The lines converge at the vanishing point in exactly the same way.

This becomes...

...this.

No matter how complicated the painting, if it attempts to create the illusion of depth, it will employ the vanishing point trick. For every object the painter wants to illustrate in depth, there will be a vanishing point. And the painter will draw his or her lines with that point firmly in mind. (Many artists use rulers to make sure of their accuracy.)

Abstract perspective. Make things recede without drawing anything recognizable.

Beach balls, beach balls, beach balls, beach balls, beach balls...

Windows into Perspective

Each of these boxes has a horizon line in it, and a vanishing point already provided. Start with your pencil sketch, then go to your colors and fill each box with a scene drawn in perspective and headed for the vanishing point. (Suggestions? Railroad Line, Yellow Brick Road, Barbed-Wire Fence, Abstract Shapes with No Conceivable Title.)

Point of View Play Time

Change yourself into a mouse and walk around your room. Sketch a few simple things as you see them. Pencil, cup, vase, door... Now change yourself into a 40-foot giant and do the same. Fill in your pencil sketches with color(s).

Landscape perspective tip: Things that are farther away are fainter, vaguer, lighter, and <u>bluer</u>.

Green · lawn turns bluer in the distance.

Things close up are more solid. Far away things are more ethereal.

Landscape and Perspective

In pencil, draw four or five windows on this page and fill them with simple landscapes. Note the examples and the tricks they employ. Suggested titles? Egyptian Pyramids in Flood, Volcano Island, Himalayan Foothills, Huge Parking Lot, Wildflower Meadow, Martian Golfcourse...

Tip: Don't name it until you're done.

Goofy Perspectives

Joe, the little fish, contemplates his future.

Painting a Still Life

When you take a bit of the real world, like a few pieces of fruit, or a collection of tools, or a pile of books, or just about anything small and arrangeable, and put those things together in a way that pleases your eye—then you've made a still life.

For a lot of people, it takes a dose of rethinking to see the beauty of a small still life. But light and shadow play on a tabletop the same as they play in the depths of the Grand Canyon. And once your eyes become freshly sensitized to light, shadow, and color—as they will once you start playing with your watercolors—then you will start to find extraordinary beauty in some of what used to be quite ordinary surroundings.

Although many artists use a realistic style for their still life watercolors, an equally large number do not. In the hands of some artists, a bowl of fruit may end up looking like a shimmer of round colors. The funny thing is, a shimmer of color can sometimes look fruitier than the real thing.

Exactly how you frame or arrange a still life is something called composition. To help you learn about composition, cut out the framing page bound into the book here, then cut out its middle and hold it up to the world. Focus on some small bit of the world—the mess on your desk for example. Zoom the frame in and out to "compose" the mess. You'll surprise yourself when you discover, as most people do, that there is one particular framing that actually looks very nice. Then, when you pull away the frame, you find yourself staring at the same old desk-mess. When you start to paint your still life, use the framing, or composition, that you like the most.

A Still Life in Four Steps

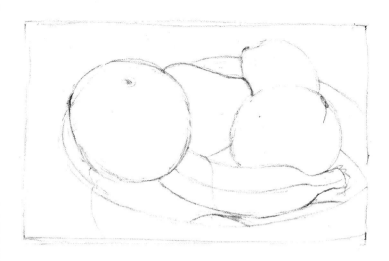

1. Rough outlines in pencil.

2. Figure out where light is coming from.
   Draw shadows with pencil.

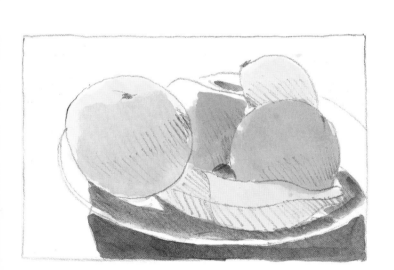

3. Add some color. Smush it around.
   Use very little paint.

4. Add details. Darken shadows.
   Layer colors on top of each other.
   Stop when it's not quite done.
   Lots of pictures are ruined by
   overworking, especially watercolors.
   I added a dark background
   to make the fruit stand out.

60

Insert scissors here...
... and cut out frame.

Cut here.

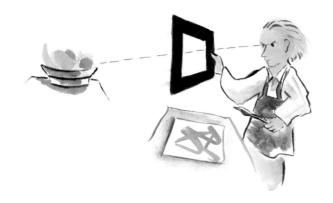

Close-up

Extreme right-wing
still life (I added
the window for balance)

Ultra close-up

The lonely still life

UFO still life
(from below)

Falling out of the picture

One Fruit Bowl, Seven Compositions

Your Turn.

Frame a bit of the world around you, sketch it roughly in pencil, and start in. At this stage, make it easy on yourself by picking an uncluttered subject with simple shapes.

Look at that! Your picture has stopped a Famous Art Critic dead in his tracks!

One Still Life, Many Ways

Frame a single still life and then try it in four or five different ways. The examples show some varying approaches. There are millions more.

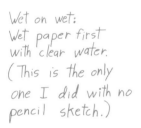

Wet on wet:
Wet paper first
with clear water.
(This is the only
one I did with no
pencil sketch.)

high contrast
black + white

flat color

dotland

The original art of
this one, like all the
others, is three times
this size.

Start with pencil
outline of flowers.
Draw thinnest
possible lines; draw
fatter lines within
flower areas.

First paint a
splatter painting...

...then add black.

A Completely Absolutely Totally 100% Blank Page

Tell a Story

It's time to give your pictures a chance to get up on the stage and tell a story. You can't think of any stories? Really? How about something like this: Introduce a character. Give a little color to its life and circumstances. Get it into trouble. Get it out.

This may seem a little bare, but on these bones hang most of the stories in fictiondom (*The Merchant of Venice*, *Curious George* and all the episodes of *Days of Our Lives*, for example). How you handle the details is the critical thing.

This is one instance where a little planning can be helpful. Dream up your character, its uniqueness and its problems before you start in. We've given you space to make two story strips. If you want, you can also make your own blank book, as we've shown here.

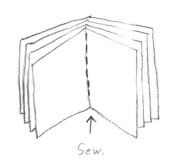

Sew.

To make a 32-page book, take 8 pieces of paper and fold them in half.

You can sew them if you want to get fancy.

Title: The Smush and the Prince

Let's start by creating
a character. For example, a smush.

This smush wanted to be a cloud,

Now create *your* character. Draw it.

What does your character want to be?

Story 1:

Story 2:

or a tree,

or a mountain.

But it was only...

 a little smush.  It tried getting a new hairdo, 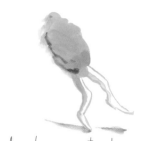 and shaving its legs. But still it was only...

What does your character do?

a little smush.

one day it wandered deep into the woods and met:

A handsome prince

Where does it go?

Uh oh! Now what?

"SMACK"

Who gave the smush a kiss.

And the little smush turned into a luscious princess,

And they lived happily ever after.

Sort of.

Saved!

All's well that ends well.